DATE DUE

DEMCO 128-8155

Bikes

From Start to Finish.

Mindi Rose Englart

Photographs by Peter Casolino

BLACKBIRCH PRESS

THOMSON

GALE

RIVERDALE PUBLIC LIBRARY DISTRICT

Detroit • New York • San Diego • San Francisco
Boston • New Haven, Conn. • Waterville, Maine
London • Munich

Dedication
To my partner, Kiva Sutton

Special Thanks
The publisher and the author would like to thank Joe Montgomery, Tom Armstrong, Liz Miller, Bill Imler, Kerry Harkleroad, and the Cannondale staff for their generous help in putting this project together.

Published by Blackbirch Press
10911 Technology Place
San Diego, CA 92127

e-mail: customerservice@galegroup.com
Web site: http://www.galegroup.com/blackbirch

Printed in Malaysia

10 9 8 7 6 5 4 3 2 1

Photo Credits: All photographs ©Peter Casolino; page 3, ©RubberBall Productions; page 17, ©Corbis; page 24, 25, ©Corel; page 31, ©Frank Hoppen.

If you would like more information about the company featured in this book, visit the Cannondale web site at www.cannondale.com

Library of Congress Cataloging-in-Publication Data
Englart, Mindi Rose.
Bikes: from start to finish / by Mindi Rose Englart; photographs by Peter Casolino
    p.   cm. — (Made in the U.S.A.)
Summary: Discusses the uses, design and construction of bikes.
    ISBN 1-56711-486-5 (hardcover : alk. paper)
    1. Bicycles—Juvenile literature. [1. Bicycles and bicycling] I. Casolino, Peter, ill. II. Title. III. Series.
TS412.E53 2002
629.227'2—dc21
             ✓I. Title
2001005815

Contents

The modern bicycle was first developed in the early 1800s. Today, you can find bicycles as far away as Tibet and as close as your own garage. In some countries, such as China, bicycles are a major form of transportation. People everywhere enjoy riding bikes for fun and exercise, in races, and to commute to school or work.

A bicycle is a simple machine, but not a simple thing to build. How are bicycles made?

Bicycles are found almost everywhere around the world.

3

Handmade in the USA

The Cannondale company has made more than a million bikes. It specializes in building bikes by hand, and is known for its unique cycling designs. Cannondale bicycles get around. The company sells its bicycles in more than 60 countries. It also sponsors athletes in some of the world's most famous and difficult races.

Opposite: The Cannondale factory is in Bedford, Pennsylvania.
Above: Cannondale headquarters is in Bethel, Connecticut.
Right: Joe Montgomery, founder of Cannondale.

5

Designing a Bike

The people that oversee production at Cannondale say that each bike passes through 71 pairs of hands before it is complete. The first pair of hands belongs to the bike designer.

A bicycle designer begins work by creating a computer model of a new bike. The design can be tested with a special computer program that simulates riding. If the bike passes these first tests, a prototype (working model) is built. As the prototype is tested, the designer makes adjustments. The designer is concerned with a bike's weight and its safety features. The bike is also checked for how it handles, and for frame stiffness (flexibility).

A mechanical engineer designs a bike (left) and examines a prototype (below).

Designing Decals

Decals are like permanent stickers. They help bikes stand out and be identified. Graphic designers create new colors and patterns for decals. These decals are applied to bikes during manufacturing. The designers get their decal ideas from nature, sports, and popular trends.

Above: A few of Cannondale's 75 bike models.
Right top: A designer looks at some printed decals.
Right bottom: Graphic designers use a computer program to create decal designs.

7

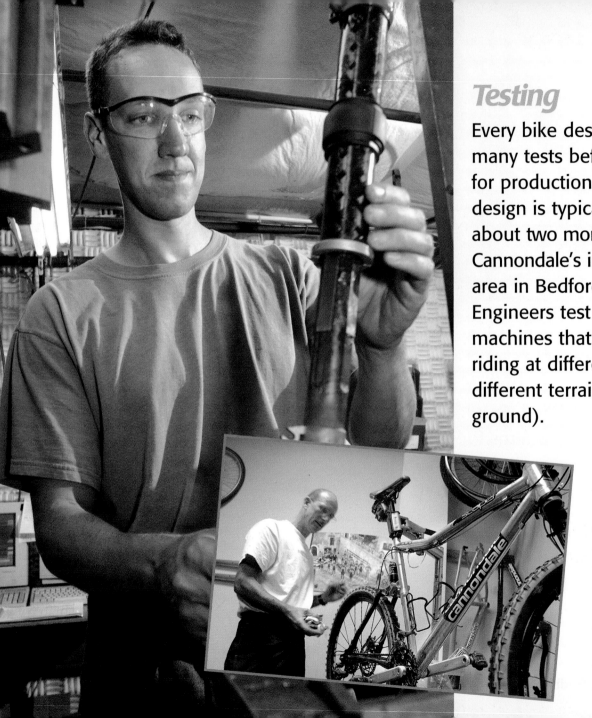

Testing

Every bike design must pass many tests before it is approved for production. A new frame design is typically tested for about two months at Q-lab, Cannondale's in-house testing area in Bedford, Pennsylvania. Engineers test the bikes on machines that simulate a person riding at different speeds and on different terrains (types of ground).

Left: *All new bikes undergo fatigue tests in Bedford. These tests show how well a bike carries small loads over a long period of time.*
Inset: *A mechanical engineer in Bethel assembles a prototype for ride-testing.*

The Warehouse

To make its bikes, Cannondale needs a lot of raw materials—especially aluminum. About 600,000 tons of aluminum parts are delivered to the warehouse each year! Before these pieces are put on the shelves, they are washed in a special detergent. This cleans them for inspection. Any pieces that have flaws are returned.

The Cannondale parts warehouse stores tons of raw materials.
***Inset:** All aluminum is washed and inspected before it is stocked on shelves.*

Prepping the Parts

Some parts are collected from the warehouse and brought to the parts prep department. Here, workers use computer-guided lasers to cut tubes and other pieces into precise lengths and shapes.

Left: *A computer-guided laser cuts a part.*
Below: *A worker punches holes in a "wishbone," which attaches to the back wheel of a bike. Cannondale produces more than 1,000 wishbones a day.*

Tab and Slot Design

The frame of a Cannondale bike is made of unique tubes. They have a special tab-and-slot design that easily aligns them for welding. A laser machine is used to cut tabs and slots.

Below left: *Cannondale builds many of their own machines. This one, called a cable guide drilling machine, makes 250 pieces out of one 12-foot piece of aluminum.*
Below right: *Cutting tabs and slots.*
Right: *After cutting, a pre-wash—called an acid etch wash—removes any dust and bits of aluminum that might interfere with welding.*

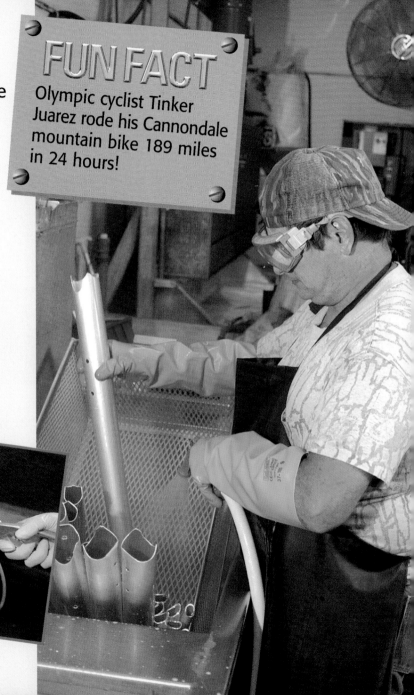

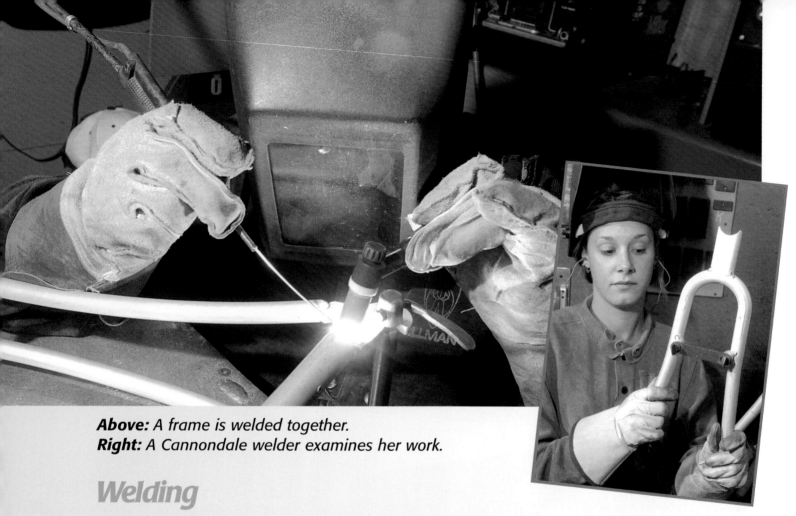

Above: *A frame is welded together.*
Right: *A Cannondale welder examines her work.*

Welding

In the welding department, different parts of the frame are welded. Welding joins metal pieces together by heating them to a high temperature. As the metal is heated, a special compound is added to the joints. Cannondale bike frames are made with "double pass welding." This process creates a very smooth joint. This type of welding takes more time, but it adds strength and durability to each bike.

Weld Sanding

After welding, all frames are sanded to smooth the welded areas. The sanding process creates a lot of dust. Workers in this department wear special suits that allow fresh air to be pumped in.

Workers in the sanding area have fresh air pumped into their special protective suits.

The Quench Oven

Welding weakens the aluminum tubes. To make up for this weakening, workers heat-treat the frames. First, a frame is heated in a machine called a quench oven. Then it gets dipped in a cooling bath and washed. This treatment may make the frame bend slightly. Workers have about 20 minutes to fit the frame back into its correct form. That's how long the frame is still soft enough to bend.

Top left: *Bike parts enter the quench oven.*
Bottom left: *Bike parts are dipped after the quench oven.*
Below left: *Parts being washed.*
Below right: *After frames and other bike parts are prepared, they go to the Unfinished Goods area (UG) for storage.*

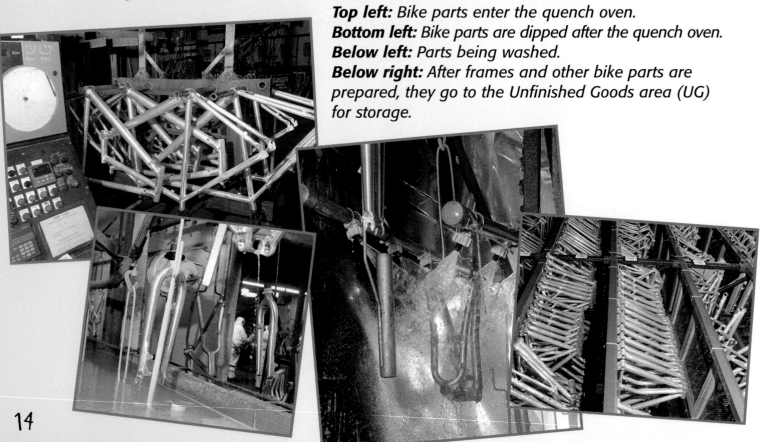

Workers in the scheduling department identify all parts needed to manufacture each bike order.

Timing Is Everything

Cannondale makes all its bikes to order. When a bicycle dealer places an order, it goes to the scheduling department. Here, information is used to create a "work instruction sheet." This sheet identifies all the parts needed to make the bikes in the order. It takes 1-5 days for an order of bikes to be built and shipped.

15

Pedaling Through the Ages

1817 Baron Von Drais invented a wooden walking machine called the Draisienne, or hobby horse. It had two same-size wheels. The front wheel was steerable, which allowed the rider to move forward in a gliding walk.

1863 The Bone Shaker, or Velocipede, was introduced. Made of stiff materials and steel wheels, this bike was literally a bone-shaker when it rode over the cobblestone streets of the day.

1870 The first all-metal machine, called an "ordinary," appeared. Solid rubber tires and long spokes on the large front wheel provided a smoother ride. This machine was the first to be called a "bicycle."

1880s The tricycle was introduced, to allow women in long skirts and corsets to ride.

1888 Tires filled with compressed air were first applied to the bicycle by an Irish veterinarian named Dunlop. The doctor wanted to give his sick son a more comfortable ride on his tricycle.

1890 Bicycles were mass-produced and bikes became a practical means of transportation.

1900 Major Taylor was the American cycling sprint champion. Taylor was one of the first black athletes to become a world champion in any sport.

1920 Kids' bikes were introduced just after World War I by several manufacturers, such as Mead, Sears Roebuck, and Montgomery Ward.

1962 The "English 3-speed" was introduced. Before the end of the decade, the 10-speed derailleur "racing bike" was the American favorite.

1986 Department of the Interior and Nielsen surveys showed that bicycling was the third most popular sports activity after swimming and general exercise.

Staging

Workers use work instruction sheets to locate parts from the Unfinished Goods area. They "stage" an order by putting all the needed parts onto a cart, which can be moved through the factory during the assembly process.

Staging carts have all the parts needed to manufacture a bike order.

A worker uses a special scanner to log each bike part into a computerized tracking system.
Inset: *An ID code is imprinted onto a bike part.*

Tracking

Each step of the manufacturing process is logged into a computer. This allows Cannondale to track how long it takes each bike to be completed. A code is stamped onto the bike at the end of the manufacturing process. This code has important information about each bike part. The code lists a serial number, and the time and day on which the bike was made. If a dealer needs a replacement part, this code helps Cannondale ship it right away.

Prep for Painting

Before painting, frames are carefully sanded again. This is called finish sanding. Once workers are sure the frames are perfectly smooth, the frame gets washed. The frame is then wiped by hand.

Left: *A frame is finish sanded.*
Below: *Frames are hand-dried and inspected.*

A worker finds the decals she needs for her order.
Inset: Decals are carefully applied to the bike's frame.

Painting and Decals

Cannondale uses a special painting process to coat its bikes. The process is called an electrostatic paint system. The frame is given a small electric charge, which attracts individual paint particles to it. This assures complete paint coverage. After painting, the bike is dried in a special oven. In this oven, the temperature reaches between 300–400 degrees Fahrenheit.

Decals are put on after the painting is complete. Workers must be very careful as they apply decals. If a decal does not stick correctly, the whole frame has to be resanded and repainted.

FUN FACT

Many celebrities, such as Madonna, Jerry Seinfeld, and Larry Bird, own Cannondale bikes.

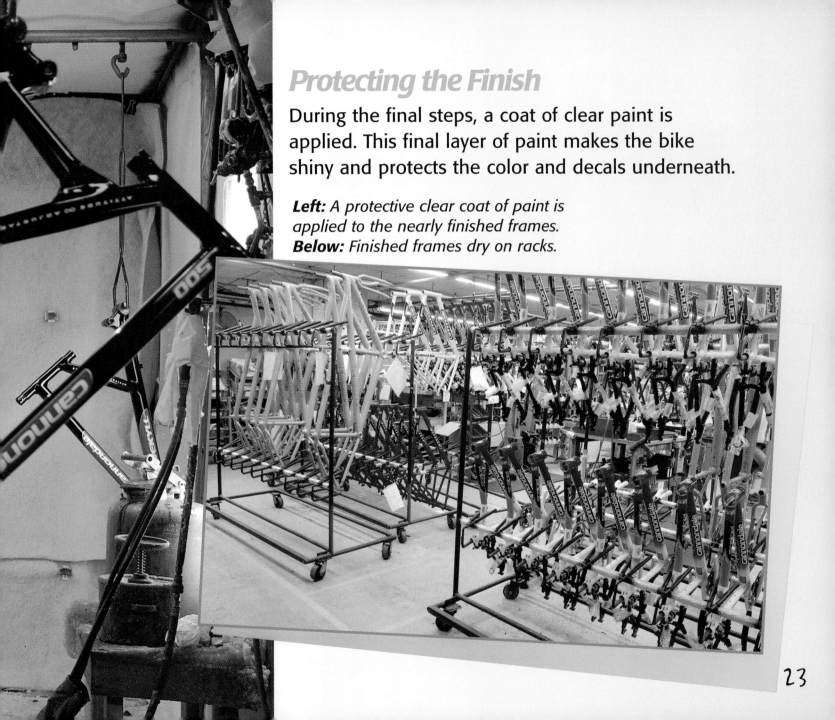

Protecting the Finish

During the final steps, a coat of clear paint is applied. This final layer of paint makes the bike shiny and protects the color and decals underneath.

Left: *A protective clear coat of paint is applied to the nearly finished frames.*
Below: *Finished frames dry on racks.*

23

Road race

Bicycle Racing

Ever since the bicycle was invented, people have challenged each other to bicycle contests. The most popular kind of contest with bicycles is racing. Today, there are many different types of bicycles. There are also many different types of bicycle racing. Here are some of the most popular kinds of racing around the world.

- **Road racing:** The most famous road race is the Tour de France. The race is roughly three weeks long, and each day requires the riders to complete a different "stage," or point-to-point race.

- **Mountain bike racing:** There are three main categories: cross-country, downhill, and dual (or dual slalom). Cross-country can be five or six laps of a six-mile course. Downhill bikers are often taken to the top of a mountain, where they race down on a marked course against the clock. Speeds in downhill can reach 60 mph. Dual involves two racers going head to head on a short, twisty downhill course.

- **Cyclocross:** Cyclocross courses have on-road portions, off-road portions, and human-made obstacles that cause the racers to temporarily dismount and portage (carry) their bikes.

- **BMX:** BMX comes from "bicycle moto cross." BMX takes place on a human-made dirt course with lots of turns and big jumps. A sub-category of BMX is freestyle, where riders perform airborne stunts.

- **Track:** Track racing contests take place on a banked oval track, called a velodrome.

Cannondale has world-renowned road racing and mountain bike racing teams. Based in Italy, the Saeco/Cannondale road racing team has won many stages in the Tour de France and several national championships. Cannondale's mountain bike racing team, Volvo/Cannondale, is the most successful team in the history of the sport. Since it was formed in 1994, the team has captured two Olympic medals, seven World Championships, and hundreds of other major wins.

Track race

25

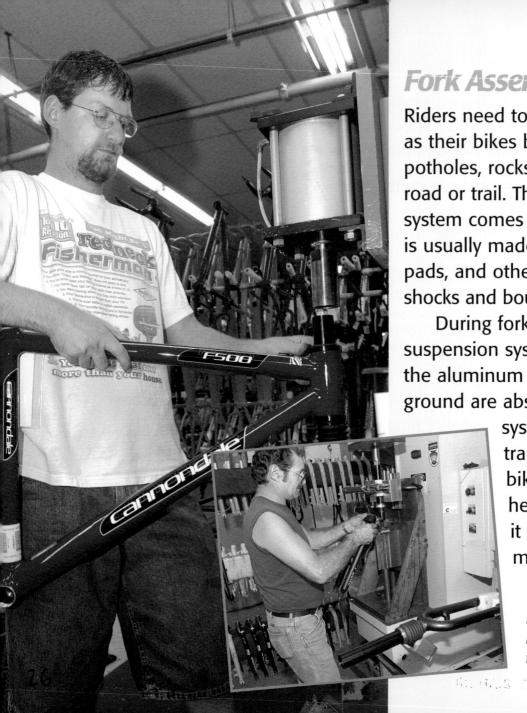

Fork Assembly

Riders need to be safe and comfortable as their bikes bounce over bumps, potholes, rocks, and other objects in the road or trail. That's where the suspension system comes in. The suspension system is usually made up of a series of springs, pads, and other pieces that absorb the shocks and bounces of road or trail travel.

During fork assembly, the bike's suspension system is put together with the aluminum fork. Shocks from the ground are absorbed in the suspension system so they are not transferred to the rest of the bike. The suspension system helps to protect the rider as it makes a trip safer and more enjoyable.

Left: *A worker creates a fork.*
Far left: *Attaching the fork to the frame.*

Wheel and Tire Assembly

Using a "lacing machine," workers insert one end of each bike spoke into the rim of the wheel and one end into the hub (center). Then the "wheel stabilizer" machine checks alignment and adjusts the tension on each spoke. An inner tube is wrapped around the outside of the rim, and the tire is fitted over the tube to make the wheel complete. After all wheels have been inspected, chain rings (sprockets) are added to the back wheels.

Far right: A worker builds a wheel by using the lacing machine.
Bottom left: Attaching the tire.
Bottom right: Attaching the chain ring.

Full Bike Assembly

At the end of the production process, all remaining parts are mounted to the bike frame. Workers assemble handlebars, gear shifters, and seats. The frame gets its fork, headset (a set of bearings that allows the front of the bike to turn easily), and handlebar assembly. Brake and shifting cables are installed. Derailleurs (parts that move the chains from one gear to another) are put on, and the crank assembly with pedals is added. The brake assembly goes onto the fork, and the chain is installed. Finally, cardboard is attached to the bike to protect the paint during shipping.

Below: *Attaching brake cables*
Right: *Preparing to attach the crank assemblage and pedals*
Opposite: *Attaching the brake assembly*
Inset: *Attaching handlebars*

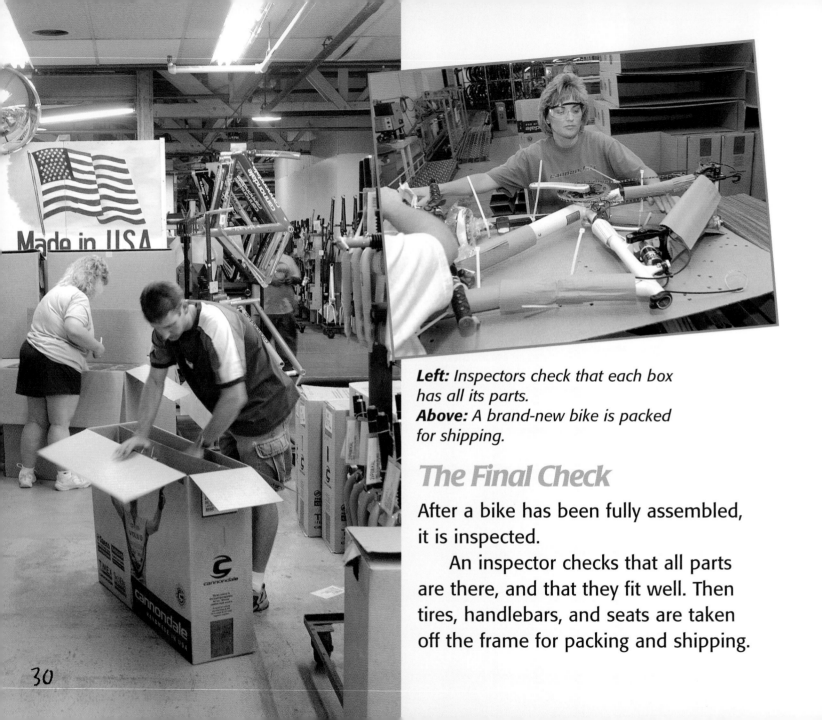

Left: *Inspectors check that each box has all its parts.*
Above: *A brand-new bike is packed for shipping.*

The Final Check

After a bike has been fully assembled, it is inspected.

An inspector checks that all parts are there, and that they fit well. Then tires, handlebars, and seats are taken off the frame for packing and shipping.

Ready to Ride

The bikes are carefully packed and stored for a brief time in the shipping warehouse. Then the trucks come and deliver them to a bicycle dealer near you. And that's where the fun begins!

Glossary

Decals Permanent stickers.

Welding Joining metal pieces together by heating them to a high temperature.

Laser A device that uses light to cut through matter.

Manufacture The act or process of producing something.

Prototype An original model on which something is patterned.

Quench oven A machine in which bicycle frames are heated in order to strengthen the frame.

Raw materials Crude matter that can be converted into a new and useful product.

For More Information

Books

Reid, Mary Ebeltoft. *Let's Find Out about Bicycles.* New York, NY: Scholastic Trade, 1997.

Erlbach, Arlene. *Bicycles* (How It's Made). Minneapolis, MN: Lerner Publications Company, 1994.

Website

Cannondale
Learn more about Cannondale and their bicycles—www.cannondale.com

Index